IT'S A DOG'S LIFE

IT'S A
DOG'S LIFE
FINDING THE PROFOUND IN THE PECULIAR

JEFF LUCAS

CWR

Dedication

To Alan and Julie Cunningham – dear, valued friends.

Acknowledgements

Huge thanks to Premier Christianity *magazine,
for their ongoing permission to rework these pieces,
many of which first appeared in the column that
I've been writing for them for the last 15 years.
Lynette and friends at CWR, it's been a while now.
Thanks for consistent friendship and partnership
in our shared commitment to the kingdom.*

Contents

Introduction   10

01. It's a dog's life   13

02. The night caller   17

03. The lookout   21

04. Offensive grace   25

05. Multi-tasking   29

06. After the flame   33

07. Shouty Church   37

08. Intimate   41

09. No U-turns   45

10. Slow down   49

11. The haircut   53

12. Offended   57

13. Scrooge   61

14. Changing the world   65

15. Five reasons to put your phone down for a while   69

16. What's that in your eye?   73

17. Twice bitten   77

18. Serving   81

19. My favourite place   85

20. Living out loud   89

21. A rite of passage   93

22. What not to say...   97

23. The power of prejudice   101

24. Together   105

25. Here is the news 109

26. Waiting 113

27. The meeting 117

28. A little means a lot 121

Introduction

It's a question that I'm often asked. Anyone who knows me, through books, preaching or both, will know that I seem to have more than my fair share of mishaps and embarrassing moments. I seem to stumble from one lash-up to another, spending much of my life crimson-faced. So when I was interviewed for a Christian magazine article recently, the journalist nervously tiptoed into the question:

Do all those ridiculous things *really* happen to you?

This was a question that thinly disguised a deeper question, one that is a little more blunt:

Are you *really* that stupid?

However you phrase the question, the answer is affirmative in both cases: Yes. Yes, I do lurch my way through life. I often wish that wasn't the case – rather, that I was known for being suave, competent, able to fill a plate at a church buffet without sending a mountain of strawberries cascading across the floor, able to exit a bathroom without first battling for five minutes with the handle of the broom cupboard.

But it's not to be.

Admittedly, perhaps I am more dedicated to noticing my endless episodes of folly, noting them, seeing the funny and hopefully the more profound side of the moment, and then sharing my gaffs with the wider Christian public.

But I decided years ago that, as a Christian leader, I was

never going to be one of those together, endlessly strong people who stand tall and secure. I wasn't going to be one of those people who have 'arrived' in life.

I've not arrived. I'm not even just on the journey. Often I'm figuratively still standing on the platform, having missed the train because I misread the timetable.

But that's OK. Leaders are supposed to be an example, but that's different to projecting a false image where we get it right all the time. And when I do share my shortcomings and sins, I don't broadcast them from a place of surrendered hopelessness – 'this is what I am, and nothing's going to change' – but rather as one who still wants to get up, dust myself down, and head where I think Jesus is heading, trusting Him to redeem my daftness. One thing I've learned about Him after all these years is this: God's primary hobby is redeeming the things that He is not the architect of – be it disaster, sin, sickness, tragedy, or the trivial follies of yours truly – He can take our ridiculousness (is that a word?) and make something rather useful out of it. Gaffs into gifts. Even trash into treasure.

And so I pray that what follows will make you laugh, cry, think, and be more hopeful – hopeful about yourself, hopeful about God, and hopeful about today as well as tomorrow.

And as always, if you've read any of my other stuff, thanks for coming back.

And if you haven't, why on earth not? ☺

Jeff

01

It's a dog's life

I've never been a fan of bumper stickers, especially the Christian kind.

Spotting that sticker that invites me to *Honk if you love Jesus*, I've obediently honked my horn, expecting to be greeted with a smile and a fraternal wave – only to be hailed by two upraised fingers that were not quite so conducive to fellowship.

And then there's the sticker that announces that *This car will be driverless in the event of the rapture*, which is silly on so many levels, it's not even worth comment.

But today, I spotted a bumper sticker that intrigued me. It simply said, *I want my dog's life*.

The car, unsurprisingly, contained a dog, confirming that canine ownership by the driver was indeed legit. I glanced at the grinning mutt that was staring back at me through the rear window of the stickered car. Its tail was wagging furiously, which apparently means it was feeling good (although there's been no recorded interview with a dog to actually confirm this theory). Its tongue was lolling, and its face was fixed in that smile that dogs sport when they're hot and their mouths are wide open.

That dog looked rather happy. For a moment, having its life seemed like an appealing idea.

Compared with us humans, dogs have it pretty easy. They have no mortgage to worry about, they go to the bathroom pretty much wherever they please, and their main work is to bark at anyone who looks remotely like a burglar.

Dogs have absolutely no idea what a prime minister, a president or a stock market crash look like.

Having a dog's life sounded rather attractive. Carefree even.

But then I thought again. These days, dogs usually exist on a diet of rather bland looking pellets, which must get old. It must be rather tedious to have to sit, fetch and beg on command, raise your paw for a treat, and sleep in a wicker basket. And then there's all the bottom sniffing etiquette that's expected whenever you meet a new friend... that's not so appealing.

'It's a dog's life' was a phrase birthed in the sixteenth century when dogs lived outside, were fed on scraps, and generally had short and fairly miserable lives. As I pondered the aforementioned sticker, I wondered – do we waste time wishing that we had somebody else's existence? We can spend our days regretting that we are not that other person who is richer, thinner, better looking, smarter, or more successful. We devour magazines devoted to photographing and chronicling the lives of airbrushed celebrities.

Are we intrigued with the well-heeled and famous just because we'd love a slice of the life that they have, which surely must be happier than our own? We ignore the Hollywood dichotomy of excess and hollowness; the reports of drug addictions and failed marriages, as our superstars lurch from one temporary relationship to another. Perhaps we think that they're the unusual ones; that we could handle fame and plenty with greater grace. But our fascination with them continues.

That craving can lead us into disaster, as we fritter our days away with ingratitude, longing for someone else's spouse, someone else's life. Perhaps that why, when God had just ten things that He wanted to say to humanity, a strong warning about coveting your neighbour's stuff appeared on the list.

But it's not just about materialism.

Recently, I've caught myself hankering for an earlier version of my own existence, back when our children were young, when life seemed so much simpler. Nostalgia paints yesterday's sky as bluer, while my free-range daydreaming pictures tomorrow's grass as greener. Endless preoccupation with what was in the past, or with what might be possible in the future, steals our ability to be fully present in today. We can find ourselves gripping hold of life so tightly that we are squeezing the life out of life.

Surely true success is found in being contented – an attitude the Apostle Paul learned to embrace. He had a rougher life than most, and would never have made the pages of our glossy lifestyle magazines. Everywhere Paul went there was a riot. Assassins pledged to kill him. He tasted deep despair. He was shipwrecked. Beaten. Falsely accused by a religious baron jealous of his influence and power. But somehow, through it all, he had learned to be content. By God, literally, I'd like to learn that lesson too. I'm asking the Lord to enrol me in contentment academy today.

Perhaps I can take a step in the right direction with this declaration: today, I don't want to be Tom Cruise, Albert Einstein, Gandhi or, if you don't mind me saying so, you.

I don't want my dog's life, my earlier life, Billy Graham's life, or the impossibly suave George Clooney's life.

Hold on.

Being Mr Clooney, just for a while, *would* be rather nice…

Oops. Back to school.

02

The night caller

So it's 1.20am, and my mobile phone rings. Loudly. A shrill ringtone, one that I selected in a moment of madness, pierces laser-like through the thick layers of my deep sleep. I wake with a start, heart pounding, eyes suddenly wide. Within a second, even before I swing my feet out of the bed, my mind springs into adrenalin-laced action, speculating wildly. Whatever has happened? Most of my friends don't phone me in the small hours for a happy little chat, which is one reason why they're still my friends.

I can't find the phone, which continues shrieking impatiently. In the darkness I bump into a rather solid piece of furniture, and utter a word of praise and thanksgiving (I wish) as I bruise myself.

As I stumble around the shadowy room at 534mph, my mind is way ahead of me, travelling at warp-factor speed, hurtling through a horrifying catalogue of possible reasons for the call. Someone in our family has been in an accident/is terribly injured/is stranded in Latvia/is lying on a cold mortuary slab, awaiting my identification. Fear creates endless chilling possibilities.

At last I locate the phone, and hear an unfamiliar voice. But the voice that is all too familiar to most of us is the niggling whisper of fear. We know it well. We're intimidated by its hiss.

Fear can speed through our minds at a rate faster than any Wi-Fi connection. Ignited and fuelled by imagination, fear is devastatingly effective at night; it mugs our exhausted minds and insists that we stay wide awake, restlessly fretting while the hands of the alarm clock crawl around the dial, silently tormenting us as we long for dawn to break. It punctuates our dreams with horror stories that drench us in cold sweat; we awake relieved, hoping it was just a dream and not a premonition.

Being afraid is something we humans do very well. Perhaps that's why, in Scripture, visiting angels usually introduce themselves with the same greeting: 'Don't be afraid'. Surely God knows that when it comes to fear, even the most faithful and faith-filled among us can fall prey to its predatory fangs.

Elijah did rather well as a person of faith, performing an assortment of exploits like summoning fire from heaven, organising the weather, and raising the dead. Most of us haven't raised the dead lately (and no, waking your teenage son in the morning doesn't count). But this man, so famous for faith, in fact ran for his life, and then prayed for death when fear stalked him. A notelet from the Cruella De Ville of the Old Testament, Jezebel, sent him and his faith packing. It was fear that took him out – a devastating smart missile.

And so, these days, I'm trying to take seriously God's oft-issued command: 'Do not be afraid'. 'Don't do that,' He says. If I'm told *not* to do something, I must have the ability, with God's help, to not go there; to refuse fear's invitations. I'm wrong to cower powerless before the Goliath that is fear. I might only have a makeshift catapult and a few stones in hand, but, by God (literally) I can topple that giant. And this is more than 'don't worry, be happy'. I need to learn to replace my anxious thoughts with urgent volleys of prayer; according to Jesus, worry produces nothing, prayer changes everything. I can place vivid imaginings of dread under arrest, taking my thoughts captive. Is it easy? No. Trust takes practice. Discipline. But just because it's easier said than done doesn't mean it can't be done.

So, what becomes of my nocturnal phone caller? It turns out that an airline, having recently mislaid my bag on a trip, has decided to return it in the middle of the night. A nice delivery chap tells me that he has my bag, and that he's just ten minutes away. Stifling a scream, I gently advise him that it's the middle of the night. It's an empty bag, I say. I have no immediate need of it. But he is determined.

He calls me three more times for directions.

Finally, at 2am, he arrives. I have a blissful reunion with my bag, and treat it like a returning prodigal. I'd missed it so. I thank him warmly – he was just doing his job.

And as I wander back to bed, I realise that my fears,

so vivid and terrifying just a minute or two ago, were quite groundless.

They usually are.

03

The lookout

Halfway down the stairs
is a stair
where I sit.
There isn't any
other stair
quite like it.

So wrote A.A. Milne in his poem 'Halfway Down', his words made all the more famous by Robin the frog. Recently, I've found myself humming that little ditty most Sundays when I show up for church (although it's not part of our worship set… yet).

It because that's where I always find my friend Larry. He'll be parked in his usual place, halfway down the stairs in the entrance foyer of our church. He's standing, though, not sitting, because he's a man on a mission.

Larry has been rather good with missions impossible,

embracing challenges both large and small. An extremely minor mission of his involves him cutting my hair. A gifted hairdresser, he is usually given more to work with than I can offer, but he manages to do the best job humanly possible with the shrinking peninsula I call my hairstyle. But his hairdressing has led to some life-altering, church-transforming encounters.

Decades ago he was the stylist for Nicki, a beautiful but slightly lost girl who was paying her way through college by removing her clothes for ogling men at a local strip club. I've written about Nicki elsewhere, but her coming to our church triggered the beginning of a wonderful, messy influx of people who were rather more obviously lost than most lost people. There's no doubt that the huge growth in our church was launched by Nicki's arrival and immediate, dramatic conversion. These days, when asked how our church grew, I rather naughtily comment that we got a stripper in.

All of that was almost thirty years ago. Yet Larry, now a sprightly 71-year-old who wears trendy clothes and sports a cool white goatee beard, refuses to live on yesterday's stories. And so he parks himself on the landing, halfway down those stairs, because he's on the lookout. He scans the teeming crowd of gathering worshippers, searching for the people that he's invited to come to church during the week. Then there are new Christians that he's informally discipling; folks he wants to make sure he greets; others he's on the lookout for to sit next to because they're alone, or just encourage because he knows that they've been through a rough season.

Larry hasn't had the benefit of a smooth-running life. Divorced twice, he spent a number of years living in his hairdressing salon because couldn't afford a business *and* a home. But he has no time for looking back or, for that matter, endlessly looking forward. He's committed to a laugh-out-loud attitude towards each new day that comes, living in the here and now, soaking up the gravy from the plate of each moment. And that means giving rather than grabbing. This caring people-watcher could be forgiven for wanting his own space at the weekends, seeing as he spends his days chatting with one client after another while he attends to their hair. But often I'll find him sitting in two services, singing the same songs, listening to the repeated message, because from his stairway vantage point, he's spotted someone in need of company.

Years ago, Led Zeppelin sang about a lady who was buying a stairway to heaven. But those who follow Jesus know well that all the trillions in the world wouldn't buy a stairway to that place. Instead, the way has been made open by the Jesus who came down, down and down again, navigating the inexplicable gap between the throne of heaven and manger of Bethlehem, opening the way by grace alone. That same Jesus went on the lookout for unlikely people like Peter and John, outcasts like Zacchaeus, and people who felt their souls were terminally stained, like the woman at the well.

So here's to Larry, and many like him, who live life on the lookout, scanning the crowd for someone who needs a smile.

I'm not at the bottom,
I'm not at the top;
so this is the stair
where
I always
stop.

Keep doing that, Larry. Keep stopping and looking.

04

Offensive grace

It's been a rather odd 24 hours. I've been sworn at by half a dozen different people, none of whom know me or each other, but apparently despise me nevertheless. I've received three messages from one young mother telling me that I made her sick to her stomach, and I surely couldn't be a parent of children. And in one particularly vitriolic email, I've been advised that I'm as bad as a child molester. If you're wondering what horrendous crime I've committed, it's simple. On Facebook, I requested prayer for a newly incarcerated prisoner, who is just beginning a prison sentence. As far as I know, he's never been in jail before.

His name is Rolf Harris.

In the wake of the monstrous abuses committed by Jimmy Saville, society was understandably appalled at the revelations about the previously iconic Harris. Perhaps our capacity for hatred is increased when someone we love dearly betrays us, and so news that the jaunty painter and presenter was actually a serial predator was devastating. And so it was with a nervous heart that I made this post:

This is likely to create some reaction, but I feel compelled to write. My request is simple – pray for Rolf Harris today, as he is sentenced. Before picking up that stone or firing off an angry response, let me be clear: what he has done is utterly evil and reprehensible. Not only is he a child abuser, but he has allowed his victims to suffer more by not admitting his guilt and forcing them to relive their terror in court. Justice must and should be done. I offer not a single word of defence for these terrible crimes. Utmost in our minds must be prayers for his victims and those who perhaps have still not been heard. Our prayers are with countless others who are still in a situation of ongoing abuse, who long for liberation and justice. But I return to one core question: Does God love Harris; did Jesus die for him? The answer is yes. And so, as he experiences utter hostility and loneliness and fear today, we should pray for him, that somehow, in some way, he might discover Christ in the midst of this dark day.

I was stunned by the response. The posting hit over 27,000 Facebook pages. There were hundreds of comments, and over a thousand people clicked 'like'. The post was republished by Christian radio stations and news websites. The vast majority of people were supportive and in agreement with the call. But I was not prepared for the angry eruption from the few.

Some of the anger came from so-called 'trolls', who just like to pick an online fight. Perhaps some were reacting out of their own bruising experiences at the hands of their own abusers. And some of those who reacted so spitefully were probably not believers, and therefore might not have understood that prayer for someone is not about approving or excusing what they did. I was careful not to mention forgiveness – for one thing, only those that have been hurt by Harris can forgive him.

But I repeat the call to pray for prisoner Harris, not least because his heart and mind need to change. However, this is not just a prayer for change in him so that no more vulnerable people might be exploited, but comes because the grace of God is so utterly stunning. Years ago, I used a phrase in a sermon, describing grace as 'outrageous'. Songwriter Godfrey Birtill was present during that talk, and went on to write the song 'Outrageous Grace', which beautifully captures something of the wondrous love that God has for each and every human being. If grace is not amazing, it's not grace.

But grace is offensive at times, because it means that God likes people whom I want Him to hate. Like Jonah, who stomped out of the revival town that was Nineveh because God was offering mercy to a hated people group (who were on the map for skinning people alive), I'd like God to show mercy to relatively nice people (like me, at least in my estimation), and nuke the Hitlers, Stalins, and Yorkshire Rippers of the world.

But the confusing, glorious truth is that Jesus made a continuous habit of hanging out with the wrong people. Like the woman caught in adultery. Zacchaeus, the tax fraudster.

A thief dying on the cross next to His.

    Like you.

    Like me.

    And like Rolf Harris.

05

Multi-tasking

The message that popped up on my computer screen seemed innocuous enough, announcing that it was time for my software to be updated. A single mouse click would launch the procedure. Usually I pause before performing this kind of techno-task, and ensure that my precious data is safe by backing it up. But that day, I was working on about ten projects at once. Without thinking, I clicked.

Big mistake.

Two hours later, I was left holding a laptop that was damaged beyond repair, my hard drive obliterated, my data wiped out. Book manuscripts, accounts, emails – they were all vaporised. I wish I could report that I responded to this crisis with quiet repose, affirming that the Lord gives, and the Lord takes away. Instead, I believe that my scream was overheard on Jupiter.

I spent three days with a 'genius' who valiantly tried to help me. I won't name the computer company – that would be quite wrong. Besides, I like the design of the piece of fruit that adorns my laptop, even if it is now only useful as a doorstop.

A few days later I popped into a toilet in the motorway services, and having washed my hands, I stood for thirty seconds with my hands outstretched in a worshipful position, waiting for the hot air to dry them. And then the truth dawned: I was actually waiting in vain for a *vending machine* to dry my hands. Passers-by were bemused by the chap who seemed lost in adoration before a silver box that dispenses contraceptives and breath mints. Awkward.

Both of these episodes happened because I was multi-tasking. Texting while I was walking into said motorway toilets, I had paused my texting to answer a call, and then got an email. Focused I most certainly had not been.

Unfocused and distracted is what most of us are. Allegedly, most people who use a tablet (such as an iPad) do so while watching TV. Half of tablet users will visit social networking sites while in front of the goggle-box, two thirds will check their emails, and most will be browsing other sites – all while watching TV. According to one academic, we're living in the age of 'infomania'. Armed with a smartphone that also serves as a camera, calculator, stock market scoreboard, web browser, email inbox, gaming console, appointment calendar, voice recorder, guitar tuner, weather forecaster, GPS, texter, tweeter, Facebook updater, music-player and torch, we're constantly multitasking. While having lunch with friends, we surreptitiously check to see what our other friends are doing, and even post photographs of the cheese and pickle sandwich that we're snacking on so that the universe can stand amazed in awe and wonder.

And although we think we're doing several things at once, multi-tasking is a powerful and diabolical illusion. Earl Miller, a neuroscientist and one of the world experts on divided attention, says that our brains are 'not wired to multi-task well… When people think they're multi-tasking, they're actually just switching from one task to another very rapidly. And every time they do, there's a cognitive cost.'[1] According to a study at the University of Sussex, constant multi-tasking actually damages your brain. They found out that people who regularly engage in multitasking have lower brain density in the region of their brain responsible for empathy, cognitive control and emotional control. Other studies have found that multi-tasking reduces your productivity by 40%.[2] Turn things off. Turn off your phone once in a while. Turn off browser notifications. Turn off email notifications. You can attend to all of those things later. You don't need them *right now*.

Why not build 'technology breaks' into your schedule, both at work and at home? To be the most beneficial, these should be for a minimum period of one to three hours at a time. This enables you to engage with people or tasks in deeper and different ways. It's also recommended that we avoid all screens (which stimulate far more than they relax) for the first and last hour of the day, so that we can begin and end with uncluttered focus.

Oops, my phone just beeped, demanding my instant attention. And although it takes the greatest effort, I've made a decision.

It can wait.

[1]Larry Kim, writing for *Inc.* (Article found at www.inc.com – accessed December 2016)

[2]Article found at www.eurekalert.org (accessed December 2016)

06

After the flame

London, 2012.

It was a golden, silver and bronze summer, untarnished even by the prelude of a three-week monsoon that made us fear a washout. Nothing could dampen the atmosphere of exhilaration that the games brought. The nation, by and large, happily succumbed to sporting fever as we enjoyed delirious days like Super Saturday, the like of which we may never see again. But even before the cosseted flame was finally extinguished, commentators were chattering nervously about post-Olympic depression, fearing that when the games went dark, our national mood would turn gloomy too. 'I can't believe it's all over,' one television pundit lamented, fighting tears. And the athletes had to face the harsh fact that, for most, the pinnacle moment of their lives was now confined to the rear-view mirrors of their memories. Dubbing the after-games hangover as POSD (Post-Olympic Sadness Disorder), the glumness that follows glory was summed up by athlete Taraje Williams-Murray: 'Ordinary life is a lot different than viewing the world from the lofty vantage point of Mount Olympus… nothing feels like it can go back to normal.'[1]

Something similar can happen to believers after they've attended a mammoth Christian event, but then have to embrace life as usual again. When the great spring and summer festivals have come and gone; the Springtime Harvest has been gathered; many thousands of Souls have Survived, and Keswick is serving scrumptious cream teas again rather than lashings of luscious Bible teaching… Life after a Christian knees-up can feel decidedly dull.

Of course, some grumpy souls insist that the event culture creates irrelevant, frothy jamborees, muttering that they prefer to stay home to continue at the coalface of serving their communities. Bah, humbug. Surely the Lord has always called his people to gather at feasts and festivals, because they help us to gather around God in unified faith, remember who we are, immerse ourselves in the big story, recalibrate our values, celebrate, and recommit. Oh, and have fun. I worked with Spring Harvest for three decades because I utterly believed (and still do) that it has a vital contribution to make in the realignment and refreshment of the Church.

That said, some returning pilgrims do get mugged by the blues. Worshipping in that tiny, out-of-tune congregation accompanied by that rickety, out-of-tune piano is not as thrilling as praising with thousands. And, much as we'd like to, we just can't take Tim Hughes home, stand him in the corner of the lounge beside that rather strange lampshade, and yell,

'Give us a tune, Tim!' every time we feel a little morose.

But there's a truth that we need to face if we are to make friends with our more mundane days, which is what most of our days are. It's a fact that I'm nervous to state, but here goes: *Jesus is not always exciting.*

Some Christians insist that Jesus is endlessly thrilling, and therefore those who are friends with Him should experience an endlessly exhilarating jaunt; a hop, skip and jump from one supernatural experience to another. But I'm not sure that I completely agree.

When Jesus was on this earth, He certainly provided some thrilling episodes. Marble-cold corpses suddenly took possession of a pulse. There was that in-your-face encounter with a screaming demoniac, which led to deliverance for him, and drowning for a herd of stampeding pork. The trio that was Peter, James and John witnessed metamorphosis on the Mount of Transfiguration. Blind eyes blinked and opened. All heady, exhilarating stuff.

Indeed, Jesus certainly isn't dull – He is fascinating, intriguing, and surprising. It was Albert Einstein who said, 'I am enthralled by the luminous figure of the Nazarene... Jesus.'[2] But perhaps His friends didn't always find Him *exciting*. Hungry for the thrills of fame, prestige and power, two of them asked Him for thrones, one at His right, one at His left – and He turned them down. His invitation to them to Gethsemane was to an endurance test – and they yawned repeatedly and fell asleep. Life with Jesus frequently got difficult and exhausting. One time the disciples affirmed their commitment to Him with a shrug-the-shoulders sigh of resignation: 'To whom shall we go? You have the words of eternal life' (John 6:68).

Today, we do not walk with Jesus as they did, but rather navigate our days by faith. Yes, there are breakthroughs. Answers to prayer. Episodes that seem to sparkle with divine intervention. But the Bible is clear: faith is not just about miracles, but also the miracle of endurance; when we feel little or nothing; when God seems very distant, but we trust anyway. Let's resist the myth that our emotions must always endorse our worship, that our feelings will always add an *Amen* to the truths we affirm. The gospel is not just true because I *feel* that it is.

Being addicted to excitement is spiritually immature. But when a Christian says that they're moving church because their 'spiritual thirst is not being satisfied', or that they 'just need more excitement', we often bow to their assumed spirituality. We need churches that can be boring, because life often is – churches that are filled with people who are committed to each other, and are not just together for the thrills and chills.

God, give us grace to be Olympian believers, who know that the stadium event is but a fractional moment; that most of life is about running marathons in the rain, doing what's right rather than what we want, and being faithful during the duller days when no one, save One, is applauding.

---

[1]Originally featured on the personal blog of Taraje Williams-Murray, found at www.taraje.com

[2]Quote supplied by www.goodreads.com

07

Shouty Church

It was a provocative slant on the Easter story.

Last April, broadcaster and journalist Janet Street-Porter made a poignant observation about the society we're becoming, and suggested that we're using technology like a rabble of loud bullies.

Writing in *The Independent*, she lamented that 'If Jesus had been tortured and crucified today, photos would be online within seconds, along with jokes and "funny" videos. Social media enables us to fight social injustice and shine a light on acts of terror, but it has also turned us into yobs – people who rarely think of the consequences before pressing the send button.'[1]

Her comment came after she had crossed verbal swords on the BBC's topical programme *Question Time*. Ms Street-Porter quickly came under smartphone fire, receiving a volley of hundreds of abusive texts, insulting her looks, tagging her as stupid, and suggesting that she deserved to die from cancer. She went on to ask a pertinent question, which surely demands our attention: 'Modern technology has turned us into a shouty society. Are we losing our ability to politely disagree?'

The evidence is in. She's right. With one in three teachers saying that they've been bruised by text and internet bullying from students and parents, we're in danger of becoming a culture where the person who yells poisonous vitriol the loudest wins. But when dialogue is replaced by diatribe, we all lose. Truth is not found when opponents just parry with soundbites. We must journey in rugged but respectful debate if we are to arrive at helpful conclusions.

But this virus of word-pummelling is not just infecting our wider culture, it is contaminating the Church too. Those of us who profess to follow Jesus need to get our own houses in order. During the 'Brexit' referendum in the UK, there were some Christians who traded rude, derisory comments on Facebook, perhaps thinking that we can suspend our commitment to measured speech and kindness when the conversation comes around to politics. Some Christian leaders posted statements that were loaded with generalities and simplistic solutions, implying that anyone who didn't share their political viewpoint was idiotic, selfish, fascist/communist, or simply just out of step with God. Obviously some policies don't reflect what God wants, but kingdom justice doesn't come when there's more heat than light. When we arrogantly insist that we have carte-blanche divine endorsement for our views, rather than robustly arguing our case, we take the easy way out and just duck behind God, or so we think.

A few days after said referendum, the Archbishop of Canterbury, Justin Welby, gave a speech that included the sad admission that some of the worst hate-mail he receives comes from Christians. 'The reality is that we do not as faith groups in our society always exhibit that secure tolerance to each other that enables us to speak powerfully of secure tolerance to the world around us. Christians are as bad as anyone at this – in fact, if I dare to be competitive, I think we're worse.'[2]

The phenomena of ranting believers is not new in America. Politicians on Capitol Hill have long remarked that evangelical Christians are among the rudest of their constituents, USING CAPITAL LETTERS AND EXCLAMATION MARKS without restraint (!!!!!!!!!), and threatening the fires of hell if their political representative doesn't vote as they demand. Genuine passion can have an unfortunate side effect – we shout. But concerns expressed at high volume or with a harsh tone don't only wound those on the receiving end, but lose their credibility. It's difficult for a politician to believe that constituents are authentically loving and caring if they act like blustering bigots, hollering insults.

And you don't have to be a vitriolic internet troll to become a verbal bully.

Those of us who are church leaders can adopt a troll-like posture when we demonise someone in the congregation because they bother us with awkward questions. When we tag a questioner as difficult, it's not long before they graduate to divisive, and although we don't actually get around to burning the witch, we certainly shred their reputations with a few words of pious dismissal. Regrettably, I've done this. It's cowardly behaviour.

At the end of his authentic and humble speech, Justin Welby offered a challenge for us all: 'Can we model confidentiality, transparency and genuine respect for one another?'

I really hope we can.

[1]Janet Street-Porter writing for *The Independent*, 3 April 2015. To access the article, go to www.independent.co.uk and search for 'shouty society'. (Article last accessed December 2016)

[2]Archbishop Justin Welby's speech, given 6 May 2015, can be found at www.archbishopofcanterbury.org (search for 'board of deputies dinner').

08

Intimate

In my extensive personal history of gaffs and lash-ups, this was surely one of the worst.

I've put my foot in my mouth so many times, I've developed a taste for leather. Like asking the lady when her baby was due when it had arrived weeks earlier. Or meeting a fellow hospital visitor at a bedside, and asking, 'So you're the patient's mother, are you?' then learning that she was in fact her sister. If blushing with embarrassment was an Olympic sport, I'd get the gold.

But this particular episode was epic in a truly terrible way. I still cringe at the thought of it.

A diminutive, nervous-looking chap approached me at the end of a service, requesting prayer. Introducing himself hesitantly, he shared his painful dilemma. 'Nobody seems to notice me,' he whispered, his eyes downcast. 'In social gatherings, I seem to be invisible. I'm awkward with conversation. Perhaps I'm boring. Nobody ever calls me by name. Would you pray for me?'

You might have guessed where this is going. Here was I, standing before a man who felt unnoticed, and for the life of me, I couldn't remember his name. Breaking into a panicked sweat, I racked my brain to try to remember how on earth he had introduced himself to me – but without success.

Christian leaders have tactics for moments like this. When unable to remember someone's name, one can pray for 'my brother', 'this child of Yours that You love, Lord', or 'my dear friend'. A Christian writer friend (it would be wrong to specifically mention Adrian Plass) froze when he was asked to sign a book for a lady whom he knew very well – but had completely forgotten her name. 'Remind me,' he murmured, using his pastoral voice, 'how do you spell your name again?' She smiled, knowingly. 'It's easy,' she replied. 'It's P-A-M.'

Awkward.

So, in that panicky moment at the front of church, I resorted to one of these emergency strategies, asking God to bless this 'priceless man that You love, know and care for'. I don't know if he noticed my failing to name him in the prayer. To this day, I hope he didn't.

We all long to be seen, to be known. Eden is a picture of naked innocence, of knowing God and each other completely. I'm not proposing nude fellowship, naturist small groups – that would surely be horrific – but the longing for self-disclosure and intimacy lingers. From the earliest days of childhood, when we master the use of the potty, wobble successfully on the two wheels of our bike, or learn to spell our names, we're desperate for someone to *see* us. We crave being noticed.

'Look, Daddy!'

'Look at me, Mummy!'

Our hunger for intimacy remains. That's why Mark Zuckerberg is a billionaire. Facebook and other forms of social media offer the opportunity for connection, however fleeting or trivial.

So let's intentionally build relationships of substance. We do this as we consciously listen, ensuring that we're not just using what others say as an opportunity to think about what we're going to say next. To be truly heard is a rare luxury.

We can transform the culture of friendships, marriages, and churches as we offer appreciation and encouragement, and pause for kindness.

And while small talk is a vital component of relationships (we can't and shouldn't go deep with everybody), we can dive beneath the surface with a precious few, and take the risk of vulnerability.

Of course, nearness is not always comfortable, or welcome. Just a few days ago, I found myself in the bowels of a tiny commuter aircraft, off on another ministry trip. The seats were tiny, and I was seated next to a very large man who made Goliath look like a pixie. With regards to his aircraft seat, his cup overflowed, so to speak. My face was flattened against the window, and he was fighting a losing battle with flatulence.

And then he turned, looked at me, smiled, and said, 'I like closeness.'

Yikes.

09

No U-turns

It all started when I lost my feet.

Unable to see them because of the partial eclipse of a spreading abdomen, and becoming quite breathless after navigating a single flight of stairs, I decided to get fit.

Everything changed overnight. Now I said 'no' to hamburgers and fries, which I previously welcomed with opened arms (or more accurately, a wide open mouth). My refusal was occasionally accompanied by tears, because I was quite attached to my junk food. Pizza was out; broccoli was in. Soon I was running four miles daily, and even visited the gym for more than conversation. Forty pounds gradually melted away. I actually overdid it a little – that's my tendency. I knew I was looking a little gaunt, because strangers would offer me food, and friends asked me how long I'd been ill. For seven beautiful years I kept it up, and even fell into the sin that so easily entangles the feet of the healthy: lithe and smug with it, I started to look down on others who were chunkier and out of condition. I lost fat, but gained the flabby haughtiness of a superior attitude.

But in recent years, I slacked off. My backsliding was gradual, and so unnoticeable. I fell for the seduction of sticky, fat-laden puddings. Real ale is surely the nectar of heaven, but when it comes to expanding the waistline, it's a witches' brew. What had been an exercise regime became an occasional pastime, and my running shoes grew pale because they saw so little sun. A little cheese here, a cheeseburger there, and before I knew it, I was heading back into the obese zone.

And that's exactly what can happen to faith. It can suffer gradual, slow, imperceptible erosion.

People don't usually suddenly lose their faith (although that does happen, especially when pointless tragedy strikes), but often just mislay it, and then can't for the life of them think where it's gone. Instead we drift, lulled into believing that cruise control works for believing, which it does not.

Much has been made of the announcement by Bart Campolo (son of Tony) that he has abandoned his Christian faith, and become a humanist chaplain. Tragically, a few internet heresy hunters (some of them little better than Bible-waving trolls) seemed to lick their lips with delight at his 'coming out'. Others have written more compassionately about Bart's exposure to the terrible pain of inner-city ministry, and his lonely wrestling with doctrines that, to him, became implausible. I was impacted by his candid confession that his faith 'died of a thousand cuts'. Ever so slowly, this bright, brave warrior was worn down. Faith drained from him, not in a breach that caused a deluge, but drip by drip, until the tank was finally empty.

All of this makes me pray that Bart will once again be overwhelmed by the authentic love of the living Christ – and that you and I will intentionally guard and nurture the faith that is our own.

Just as a diet is simply the organised monitoring of what we eat, and an exercise programme is about mapping out a realistic strategy for fitness, so we are taught to take faith one day at a time, and to pray for daily bread. The past can help us – that's why Israel was repeatedly commanded to build monuments, write things down, and record the acts of God among them – but while the present can be fuelled by the past, faith must be re-energised and even recommitted to today.

Without that diligence, believing turns into a rather dull, grey habit, and churchgoing and all the accompanying Christian stuff looks flaccid and unattractive. Ironically, that's when we really need the Church, so that we can huddle together and affirm the truths we believe, especially when we don't feel like believing them.

It means that I will pray today, and not just vaguely believe in the power of prayer. For decades I had decried the 'quiet time' as legalistic oppression – and became a pauper as a result. I've changed my mind.

And faith demands that I will hang in there when God is unnervingly quiet, especially when He seems extremely chatty with others.

I'm glad to report that I'm back on track with the fitness

programme and healthy diet. The surplus pounds have gone again. I'm even wearing an electronic band to monitor my daily exercise and calorie intake. I've decided to keep it in check. I've *decided*.

And, while I'm at it, I have decided to follow Jesus. Today.

By the grace of God, no turning back.

No turning back.

10

Slow down

I stared at the envelope, and tried to halt the rising feeling of dread that sickened my stomach. Adorning one corner of the stern brown stationary was the logo of the Surrey Constabulary. Meldrew-like, I could not *believe* it. I had been caught speeding yet again, the hapless target of a speed camera.

I won't make light of my crime – speeding kills people, and I was guilty. Never mind that I was only four miles per hour over the limit – I was speeding.

Last time it happened, I was forced to attend a speed awareness course. A sorry, ashamed-looking group shuffled into a lecture room for a three-hour event designed to show us just how devastating speed can be. I actually rather enjoyed the experience, and stayed behind afterwards to thank the instructor for a good evening. He responded by looking at me as if I was quite mad. I graduated from the course (which was no great achievement, because all you have to do is show up), and vowed that I'd slow down (a pledge that I clearly couldn't honour, given the arrival of this latest sad, brown envelope).

I live my life at speed. I eat quickly, and I can't think why. Savouring the flavours of food has never been my style. I wish I could say that I was raised in a large, hungry family, where if you didn't eat your chicken quickly, it would be snatched off the plate – but it's just not true. I just race through my food, because I race through everything. I speed-read, preferring to skim over sentences rather than fully digest the words. I multi-task, steam through to-do lists, and fume in rush-hour traffic jams, where congestion means that the one thing you can't do is rush. I get things done, so that I can get on to the next thing. But there's always something else to do, somewhere else to go, some other experience that demands that, whatever I'm doing, it won't be for long.

Lately, I've been asking myself: why the haste?

Rushing is an unconscious habit, and one that's hard to break. I dash without thinking. I don't have to be late, under pressure, or behind schedule in order to be in a hurry. Slowing down takes conscious effort. In a world of fast food and high-speed Wi-Fi, it's easy to just go with the flow, even if the flow is a torrent rather than a trickle.

And then I rush, simply because I always have. It's my default setting. I've no idea how long my mother was in labour when I came into the world, but I do know that I arrived early – very prematurely. Perhaps I took minutes rather than hours to make my appearance, and having received a slap from the midwife, I proceeded to ask when school would be starting.

Then there's the subtle pressure to be busy, because haste offers proof that we are in demand; that those who need us must get in line or take a number.

Why is slowing down is so hard? When I relax, I feel guilty. Going on holiday takes serious mental and emotional preparation. Suddenly finding myself without activity, and the rush created by rushing, I can spiral down into vague depressiveness, enduring rather than enjoying those lazy days of sunshine.

But as the speed awareness course demonstrated with horrifying illustrations, speed is truly devastating, and not just on the roads. I've made super-swift decisions that proved to be disastrous, and many messes that could have been prevented with some pause. I've wasted too many beautiful moments because I've not been fully present in them, quickly dashing on to the next thing, thinking it would be better (which it invariably isn't). Life lived like that becomes something to get through, rather than an experience to savour.

If I want to become more like Jesus, then a better rhythm won't be a luxury, but a necessity. He knew how to say no; at times He evaded the madding crowds, and commanded His friends to come apart for a while, presumably so that they wouldn't fall apart.

So, wish me well as I make my attempt at slowing.

Meanwhile, I've got to go. Must get on.

Or…

…maybe not.

11

The haircut

Hairdressers often make great evangelists.

For one thing, they have a (literally) captive audience, keen to chat beyond the standard conversational fodder that they (and taxi drivers everywhere) have to endure. And then, hairdressers are trusted with the precious commodity that is hair, so clients are more likely to trust them to discuss matters of the soul.

Most importantly, hairdressers make good evangelists for one simple reason.

They're armed.

OK, so scissors have limited potential as a weapon, but in the wrong hands they can be lethal – hence, encouraging a more attentive response to a Jesus-loving stylist on a mission from God.

All this talk of evangelistic hairdressers is no theory. My hairdresser friend Larry, (whom you may remember from Chapter 3), who painstakingly tries to shape my shrinking hirsute peninsula into something stylish, is gifted at sharing the good news of Jesus with his clients.

But recently the tables were turned for me. I became somewhat evangelistic, and the chap cutting my hair was the eager listener. And this was something of an answer to prayer, because my attempts at sharing my faith over the last decade or so have been somewhat lacking. In missional terms, I had lost my voice. Reacting to the over-zealous, cringeworthy evangelistic techniques of my early years as a Christian, when I would delightedly buttonhole strangers and inflict a breathless monologue upon them (regardless of whether they were interested, intrigued or even awake), I had fallen quiet on the sharing Jesus front. And many of us have done precisely the same. Excused by the oft-used preaching quote, 'By all means preach the gospel, and if necessary, use words,' some of us have packed up using words altogether. But the chap who said that was none other than St Francis of Assisi, famous not only for chatting with squirrels, but also for giving away everything that he owned. When you've donated all you have to the poor because of your love for Jesus, you probably don't have to use that many words.

So I've been asking God to help me speak out a little more. And last week, away from home, I walked into a random, unfamiliar hairdressers, and was taken aback by the immediate opportunity I had to share my faith. So quickly did the hairdresser start asking me questions about Christianity, that I forgot to say how I wanted my hair to be cut. Enthusiastically chatting about the difference between dead religion and living faith, I was utterly distracted – and, added to that, I had removed my glasses, so I couldn't see what was happening in the mirror. Spec-less, I'm as blind as the proverbial bat (and probably blinder, given that I'm not equipped with sonic radar).

Twenty minutes later, I nervously put my glasses back on, to be greeted by the reflection of a chap who looked like a skinhead paramilitary. I knew it was *very* short because when I walked back to the church where I was speaking later that evening, a lady volunteer (who I'd met earlier in the day with a fuller complement of hair) greeted me by saying, 'Gosh. Who did that to you?' My wife welcomed me with a look of sheer horror, followed by a sympathetic smile.

But here's what happened. I'd invited the hairdresser to come to church that night, and had given him some books, expecting that he wouldn't show (oh me of little faith). But he did come. He came up to me afterwards and told me that he'd enjoyed the evening, had signed up for Alpha, and had agreed to meet the minister for coffee later that week.

I would later joke that I laid down my hair for the sake of the gospel, although there was never much to lay down. But I recovered something far better: the authentic joy of having a natural, non-pushy conversation that will hopefully help someone to discover how much God loves them.

And so, I'm getting my voice back, ever so slowly. And hopefully, one bright, beautiful day, I'll grow my hair back too.

12

Offended

I know.

I should be able to fix a flat tyre, but when God was handing out gifts of practicality (which includes the ability to repair, build, or assemble anything), apparently He passed me by. I'm useless. I own a tool kit, which looks new, mainly because I've never figured out how to use any of the tools… with the exception of the hammer. Obviously I know what that's for, silly. It's for hitting one's fingers while taking aim at a nail.

Penetrated by a rogue shard of glass, the tyre exploded and deflated in seconds. My wife Kay and I paused the marital hymn-singing that we usually engage in while driving, and I turned to my wife, a composed smile on my face: 'Darling, I do believe that we have a flat tyre. Let us praise the Lord for the opportunity to rejoice in this minor but undeniably irritating development.' She nodded an Amen.

Sadly, nothing like that actually happened. I growled

something unrepeatable, pulled the car over to the side of the road, and wrestled with the temptation to invite Kay to change the wheel while I supported her in prayer, seeing as I am so practically useless.

The wheel jack was a six-part contraption that required assembly, and was designed by a mad, demonised engineer, so I decided to abandon any possibility of fixing the problem myself, and reached for the phone to call roadside assistance.

A gruelling 27 hours later (actually two, but it felt so much longer), a smiling, practical-looking chap arrived, assured us that he would change the tyre in a jiffy (news that created both envy and gratitude in me), but then asked if I would assist. 'Cars are speeding by here, Mr Lucas. You got a flat in a dangerous spot. While I change the wheel, could you help by slowing the traffic down?'

I shelved the protest that I had not actually *chosen* to have a puncture in a dangerous place, and instead walked ten yards down the road and proceeded to try to convince fellow motorists to temporarily limit their speed. This was accomplished by holding both arms out in front of me in the posture of a diver, then waving them down together: I smiled while waving, trying to communicate that my signal was a request, not a command.

The reaction was mixed. Some kindly obliged, and applied the brakes. Others seemed bemused by the sight of this strange chap who was apparently worshipping them from the roadside. But there were those who reacted by doing the opposite of what I wanted them to do – they sped up, shook their fists, and some even yelled a few expletives as they raced by. Apparently, I had committed a cardinal offence. I had asked them to delay their progress by a maximum of two seconds. The blue touchpaper was lit, igniting phosphorus rage. They were offended.

Some go through life perpetually on the edge of offence. They are picky people who live just beneath their skin, ready to be upset if someone so much as threatens to put a kink in their day. If the plane is delayed, if the meal takes five minutes longer to arrive, if another driver cuts them up, if the sky is sullen grey, their faces turn to angry red.

And it happens in the Church, too. I've met Christians who have apparently been offended since birth. One wonders if they got irritated with the midwife, enraged by the slap on the backside that welcomed them into the world. Some may go to church just to get offended, and even seem frustrated if there's nothing to be frustrated about. Sometimes I wonder if there are people who enjoy sniffing out potential error and inconsistency, and seem delighted when others fall. I've even known some to assume the demeanour of a victim, which is ironic, given that they are the ones who engage in bullying manipulation, creating actual victims everywhere they go.

The chronically offended go through jobs, churches, friendships and even marriages like knives through butter. The sound of crunching eggshells around them is deafening: people tread carefully, eager not to stir the sleeping giant. It's surely a miserable existence.

Back on the roadside, I continued my frantic waving. And

I learned some valuable life lessons from the experience.

Don't look for opportunities for irritation.

When they arise – and they inevitably will for all those in possession of a pulse – stay cool.

And if you own a wheel jack, read the instructions right away.

13

Scrooge

I don't understand Black Friday.

Meanness is ugly. Grabbing is unattractive. And yet the annual shopping bonanza (ironically the day after Thanksgiving in the US – a day for being grateful for all that we have) inevitably triggers greed-fuelled, shopping-frenzied scuffles and scrums across the western world. In the US especially, determined ninja-shoppers will jump queues and elbow, shove and even punch each other in their relentless pursuit of a bargain. The (unreformed) spirit of Ebenezer Scrooge is alive and well. We don't have to be penny-pinchers to qualify as being stingy – we only need to insist that most of our pennies and pounds are spent on us.

In his novel *A Christmas Carol*, Dickens paints Scrooge, the wizened old skinflint, as a 'squeezing, wrenching, grasping, scraping, clutching, covetous old sinner.' Hardly a handsome portrait.

But we don't have to literally wrestle with fellow shoppers to qualify as ungenerous. We're all familiar with the awkward dance around the issue of who pays the bill at dinner (or perhaps, being honest, we're the ones that dash for the loos the second the bill is brought to the table). Perhaps you have a friend who always promises to 'get the next one' but never remembers to. Or perhaps your Christian friends are the very last people to offer to buy a round in the pub, instead choosing to nurse the bottom inch of a pint for a further hour. We can even attempt to veneer our meanness by making a virtue of it, insisting that we're thrifty, when in fact we're just being a bit tight.

All of this (sometimes masterminded) meanness not only takes a lot of effort, but actually robs us of the joy of giving. A recent sociological survey featured in the book *The Paradox of Generosity*[1] revealed that generosity is very good for us, and not in a silly, telly-evangelist, 'Give and God will make you rich' way. Research suggests that the more generous we are, the more happiness, health and purpose in life we enjoy. Generosity not only blesses others, but brings joy to our own hearts too.

And more importantly, generosity changes the world. The Early Church profoundly impacted their culture with their generous lifestyles, even though most of them were poor. In their day, generosity was not widely valued; Roman society embraced a system called *Liberates*. Simply put, the code went like this: you scratch my back, and I'll scratch yours. A tidy arrangement – unless you were poor, and had nothing to give. Widows and orphans found themselves stranded at the bottom of the social food chain.

In beautiful contrast, the early followers of Jesus gave their service, their money, their goods, their time, their safety, their creature comforts, and their reputations, with a generosity that was not just a series of isolated, unusual actions, but a way of life. They scattered good everywhere, freely and indiscriminately. They looked for sweaty feet to wash, and went even further. When terrible plagues hit and huge swathes of the population fled the cities, abandoning the sick, the Christians stayed behind, nursing the ill back to life – which meant that some of the carers died in the process.

It's been said that we are most like God when we give. Those early believers didn't just share words and ideas about God, but they showed a confused world what the giving God looks like. He's obviously a fictional character, but Scrooge changed. Dickens describes the transformation:

'Some people laughed to see this alteration in him, but he let them laugh, and little heeded them… His own heart laughed: and that was quite enough for him.'[2]

So I want to challenge us – let's choose to live generously, and not just with our stuff.

Give that stretch of tarmac to the bullish driver who rudely cuts in during the rush hour.

Offer the rare gift of listening.

Instead of fuming over the man who stands in the 'five items only' queue in the supermarket with eight items in his basket, let's smile, and wish him a pleasant day.

Let's not just believe in generosity, but think, plan, and act. Too many of us practise post-dated generosity; one day we'll get around to giving, but we mistakenly think that until we do, believing in the idea is enough. It isn't.

And if we're honest enough to admit a tendency to be tight, let's know that we can change.

[1]Christian Smith and Hilary Davidson, *The Paradox of Generosity* (New York, USA: Oxford University Press, 2014)

[2]Charles Dickens, *A Christmas Carol* (Public domain. First published by Chapman and Hall, 1843)

14

Changing the world

Barney loves grilled cheese sandwiches, stuffed teddy bears, Elvis Presley, and people.

Abandoned by his parents at birth, and diagnosed with severe learning difficulties, he spent his first 30 years in the clinical sterility of a state hospital. After a spell living in a group home, he decided to go it alone, quite unaware of his seven younger siblings who lived nearby (and they too were oblivious to his existence). He lived independently for decades.

But as someone commented just last week, Barney didn't just live downtown, he really *lived* downtown, becoming such a local celebrity that the new Post Office was named in his honour. Barney spent his days popping into shops, making new friends, and investing time in conversation. People would stop him in the street to catch up with him.

He used his networking skills to raise money for local charities, and would often be spotted strolling around town with an empty mayonnaise jar, collecting change for his latest cause. When asked what his favourite charity was, he would answer, 'All of them.'

Kathleen was a surprised widow. Her husband Jimmy, a local physician, died quite unexpectedly from heart failure. Her world shattered, but she determined to energetically press on with faith and life. Every Sunday, she can be spotted in our church, seated in the same area she always sits, wearing the encouraging smile that she always wears.

Kathleen has an endearing but rather strange habit. When she watches television, she joins in with the dialogue. If an onscreen character asks if anyone would like coffee, Kathleen catches herself joining in: 'Yes please.' She caught the habit from a friend.

Barney.

Meeting Barney during one of his downtown walkabouts, Kathleen, together with another friend, decided to invite Barney to go to the cinema with them. He was delighted, and the movie-going became a regular habit. He would often phone Kathleen many times in a day, wanting to discuss upcoming films, keen for another outing. And he would often join in with the onscreen conversation, which was a little embarrassing in a crowded cinema. When Kathleen's friend went through some personal trials, and dropped out of their little film group, Kathleen continued, and made those cinematic outings with Barney a priority.

Barney's local impact continued. When his seven siblings

were finally tracked down, and came to town to visit him, they were welcomed by the mayor of the city, and treated to a civic luncheon in Barney's honour. Not only did they have no idea that they had a brother, but were moved by the news that he was such a local treasure.

Barney died last week, and over a hundred people gathered in a city park to celebrate his memory. And last Sunday, Kathleen told me about their outings.

When she told me about their excursions, and about Barney and his downtown chats and charity work, I realised that true heroes are those who stop fantasising about the life they could have, but just get on and fully give themselves to the life that they do have. For very different reasons, both Barney and Kathleen could have allowed grief and disability to derail them, corralling them into a life of sullen self-preoccupation. But both chose a different path.

It's been said that most people spend their entire lives indefinitely preparing to live. We squander days and decades waiting for our circumstances to improve, postponing joy, ignoring opportunities for service, always waiting for the better tomorrow that never arrives.

And when life is lived on hold, not only does it turn into grey survival, but we fail to notice that, in reaching out to bless others, we bless Jesus, who made it clear: when we visit the prisoner, clothe the naked, and care for the sick, we do it for *them*, but those acts of kindness are done to *Him*. Our acts of kindness needn't be huge, grand gestures. It's perfectly possible that, with a pause for a chat, a rattled mayonnaise jar and a handful of movie tickets, we can change our world.

Today, let's look for Jesus, and show Him kindness. Somewhere in our day, perhaps heavily disguised, He's waiting.

15

Five reasons to put your phone down for a while

It's a familiar and vaguely depressing sight. We are a culture glued, stuck firmly to our smart phones. Wander through any airport, sit on any train, and you'll see hundreds of people slavishly ignoring everyone else, transfixed instead by the small screen that they clutch in their hands. Whoever thought that our gods would be small, handheld devices before which we kneel, figuratively speaking, in humble homage? Let's do ourselves a favour and dethrone that god, and give our phones a rest, for some very good reasons:

1. That little screen might be sucking the life out of you.
We tend to think that information is power – we're invigorated when we're in the know. But that's a lie. In 1988, Gordon MacDonald wrote his book *Restoring your Spiritual Passion*, and pointed out that we often live as emotionally drained souls because we're overloaded with choices and information. That was a good three years before the dawn of widespread email and internet use. Now we're drowning, awash with useless knowledge.

2. The world doesn't need to know that you like porridge.
Before Facebook, you never did call a friend after breakfast and say, 'Guess what! I just ate porridge! I've gotta hang up, got 4,377 friends to call. Bye!' The world will keep on turning if we fail to report that we've eaten, gone shopping, or have terrible bowel trouble after eating a bad packet of ham. Honest. It will.

3. While finding out about people, you're missing out on people.
Here's the news: unless you're extremely selective, those hundreds or thousands of 'friends' on Facebook are not your friends. They won't be snacking on the sausage rolls at your funeral party. But if you half-listen to the people you're with while concentrating on the souls that you'll never meet, your actual friendships will go offline at high speed. Don't miss out on engaging with interesting, colourful, needy, inspiring people in favour of the faceless (apart from a dodgy profile photo) on Facebook.

4. Life was meant to be a conversation, not a newsflash.
Twitter is most often about declaration rather than conversation, but life was never meant to be a series of pithy pronouncements made in 140 characters or less. Don't issue a press release – have a real chat instead.

5. Your phone won't feel hurt if you ignore it.
I have a friend who is wise, loving and a brilliant listener – until his phone rings, beeps or chirps. He is then compelled to answer it, even though he might be in a critical conversation with someone who is sharing a marriage crisis, a major career change, or a forthcoming amputation. There might be a person on your phone, but your phone is not a person. Take control. Be the boss. Ignore it. Being a machine, it won't get wounded, feel neglected, or withdraw into a sulky silence, not talking to you for three days. Believe me, it'll be ready to talk again whenever you are.

16

What's that in your eye?

You may remember the controversy.

Parliament was debating air strikes, and there was quite a row about a comment that the Prime Minister at the time had allegedly made, suggesting that anyone who opposed the motion to bomb was a 'terrorist sympathiser'. Describing the remark as a 'desperate and contemptible slur', members of the opposition repeatedly demanded an apology during the debate. I was irritated (OK, I was incensed), and while still in that smouldering state, I rather unwisely said so on Facebook. Sometimes I wish there was something in the Bible to warn against hasty, hot-headed use of social media – 'Strayest thou not to make a posting whilst frustrated, but go forth and post a photo of your breakfast instead' – Proverbs 94:2. (Don't look it up, I made that up.)

My sarcasm-tinged online comment stated that a simple apology would have been a good idea, and an expression of true statesmanship. A few retorts and private messages later (some from friends who also happen to be politicians), I realised that my own tone had been somewhat harsh and acerbic. The point of my writing here is not to debate the rights and wrongs of the bombing campaign, nor even discuss the PM's alleged remark. The issue for me was that my tone was that of one who had rushed to judge without knowing the facts. It would have been good to take the opportunity to call for prayer for all who give themselves to public service, whatever their party politics or opinion on this issue. I quickly deleted the post, and sent a personal message to some of my politician friends who, along with many others in parliament, had lost sleep that week over making such a difficult decision.

But then the reality hit me. In the tiny goldfish-bowl world that I inhabit as a Christian leader, I was guilty of the very thing that I had rushed to condemn another for – a hurried, thoughtless aside. And that led to an uncomfortable realisation; I needed to go to Facebook and Twitter, and apologise for my error. There's not much health in demanding that others do that which we ourselves are unwilling to do. I share this not to appear noble, but quite the opposite: in swiftly pointing the finger, I had stumbled into bruising clumsiness. As Christians, we're free to disagree (and should do so when principle is at stake), but we should disagree agreeably.

The response to my online contrition was most gracious,

which was both heartening and awkward – it's difficult to be affirmed for being a clod, even if I am an apologetic clod. But the humbling experience taught me that we humans are very gifted at seeing the faults of others, while either being blissfully unaware of our own, or just deciding to ignore them anyway.

Jesus exposed this rather absurd aspect of the human condition with a farcical word-picture, involving people painstakingly seeking to remove a speck from somebody else's eye, while clambering around with an enormous plank sticking out of their own heads. Despite such a blistering exposé of their own ridiculous condition, it seems that few of the Pharisees actually grasped what He was saying, apologised for their actions or changed their hypocritical ways.

Elton John was onto something when he famously declared that 'sorry seems to be the hardest word'. Some of us are not only oblivious to the damage that we cause, but seem unwilling to correct it when we discover that we've been hurtful. And the advice churned out by the ancient weepy flick *Love Story* is most unhelpful in this regard. The slogan that accompanied the tragic movie (which left me in tears at the end, as a solitary male in a cinema full of very stoic females) declares that 'love means never having to say you're sorry', which is just ridiculous.

None of us get it right all the time – not me, not you, not prime ministers, past, present or future, not anyone – save One. In the hectic busyness of life, and the ready availability that we all have to make our voices heard in a way that is unprecedented in history, let's watch our words, spoken or written. And when we do lash it up, as we will, let's quickly reach for the word that can bring healing and grace to all who hear it uttered, if it's offered with sincerity:

Sorry.

17

Twice bitten

Snakes. They look scary, they slither and hiss, and Eve should never have chatted with one. But living part of the year in Colorado, they're neighbours. Occasionally they stop by unannounced, which is rude. And I'm not talking grass snakes, or the apparently dodgy but elusive British adder, which I believe has only been responsible for 95 bites in the last century. In Colorado, our snakes rattle.

Recently, someone in our locality decided to impress his friends by picking up a passing rattlesnake, with a negative result. He was bitten twice. The venom surged through his veins at such speed that there was no time to get him to hospital, so he was rushed to a local veterinary practice, where he received a life-saving anti-venom injection usually reserved for inquisitive dogs.

It seems that a lot of people try to pick up snakes. In the southern states of America there are even some religious sects that include dancing with rattlers as part of their worship. Based on a terrible misinterpretation of Mark 16:18, they believe that this is a demonstration of their faith (which is ill-advised, given how many of them get bitten). They also take it in turns to sip poison, which is just downright senseless. I used to complain about the watery blackcurrant juice served up at non-conformist communion services, but after hearing about these sorts of practices, I'll never moan again. Bad theology is indeed a harsh taskmaster. Allegedly, half of all rattlesnake bites happen because someone has tried to pick them up. Virtually all bite victims are male, and 90% of the incidents are allegedly alcohol related.

This suggests two things: apparently snakes look more attractive when you've had a beer or three, and men are the main culprits by far. So why do they do it? Apparently, it's to impress. Call it macho madness, or unrestrained ego, but fiddling around with fanged ones is the habit of those who want to prove their courage.

Being seen by others is a primary human need. We want to be important; valued; missed; affirmed.

Sadly, some of us never grow out of that childlike hunger to be seen, and spend our whole lives anxious about what others think about us (which is futile, because, as I mentioned earlier, most of the time, they'll never tell us) or posturing ourselves to deliberately impress. Ironically, showing off quite often has the reverse effect, and is off-putting rather than attractive. When the focus of our conversation is us – where *we've* been, what *we've* done, and who *we've* been seen with – we paint ourselves as self-centred and even perhaps even a little bit pathetic. Posturing is counter-productive.

And this driven appetite to impress can affect our faith. Jesus picked His strongest words to rebuke the pray-and-display Pharisees, who peppered their intercessions with phrases that tickled ears and turned heads, and used makeup to make themselves look drawn and fatigued so that the world could know that they were fasting. And when offering time came around, the dropping of a coin was accompanied by the equivalent of a trumpet fanfare, as they shamelessly announced their generosity to all. Jesus called them whitewashed tombs. Blind guides. And, interestingly, snakes.

So let's beware of the temptation to advertise the good things we do. When we're tempted to casually drop into conversation our 4am prayer time, let's not bother to announce the timestamp. Look cheerful when you fast, even if you'd be willing to use violence to get your hands on a chocolate digestive. Don't wave that banknote around before you place it in the plate. Let's practise the discipline of secrecy, mugging others with kind surprises, without seeking any acknowledgement. When the opportunity to show off becomes available, let's leave it well alone.

And if you happen to come across a passing reptile, do yourself a favour, and leave it well alone too.

18

Serving

Travelling is stressful these days.

First of all, if flying, one is required to actually go to an airport. While these places are smattered with gleaming Duty Free shops with luxury goods targeted at people who don't need the discount, the fact is this: airports are places that people actually don't want to be in unless they are (a) plane spotters who wear bicycle clips in bed or (b) excited ten-year-olds. I am neither, and realise that an airport is somewhere that nobody actually wants to go to – people are only there because they want to be somewhere else. Airports are emotional black holes, crammed with people who are either: waiting (and bored), late (and panicked), or are waiting on standby to catch another flight because they missed theirs (bored *and* panicked).

Then there's security, where one has to navigate the basic assumption that you are up to no good. There are a few quite jolly security operatives who man the conveyor belts leading into those x-ray scanners, but many more are stony-faced, giving the impression that if you actually leave a bottle of water in your bag, then you are worthy of lifetime imprisonment.

And then there's the nightmare that is Baggage Reclaim. Travelling with a large group recently, Kay and I got through to the carousel first, and decided that it would be helpful to the rest of our gaggle of travellers (there were 45 of us) if we hauled all their bags off the conveyer belt. This would make things easier.

It was then that the case of mistaken identity happened. A diminutive little English lady (not a part of our group) approached me, demanding that I remove her bags from the belt and load her trolley with them. I immediately wanted to tell her that I was not in fact an airport employee, but decided it would be churlish. What was so wrong about helping this somewhat fragile-looking woman with her bag? So what if she thought I was a porter?

It was then that my resolve to serve was tested. Apparently I didn't load her bag onto the trolley in the manner in which it should be loaded, and she told me so. 'No, not like that, flat, please, flat…' She tut-tutted and huffed at me, didn't say thank you, and didn't seem appreciative in the slightest. It's been said that the only way to find out if you're a servant is to see how you react when people treat you like one.

Up and down the UK, people will turn up at churches and do what they do every weekend. They'll put the kettle on, hand out the hymnbooks, wash up the tea cups, and shake hands with visitors. The vast majority of them are unpaid, and many of them are unsung. Perhaps you're one of them, and a lack of appreciation and gratitude has left you feeling used. If you find yourself among their ranks, then please accept this, the tiniest expression of thanks that is unworthy of your sacrifice:

Thank you. Keep up the good work.

And congratulations on being qualified for the description that Jesus celebrated:

Servant.

19

My favourite place

I just got back from a trip to one of my very favourite places on planet earth. Visiting this particular destination is always refreshing – a mini-break there never fails to re-energise me. Checking in is always a breeze, and it's so very inexpensive. I go every week.

It's a birdwatcher's paradise. Any number of species can be seen dotted around, skittering about in a hurry here and there. Others gracefully swoop down to land together, a perfectly coordinated squadron.

Admittedly, there are a few drawbacks that wouldn't help this favourite spot of mine in a TripAdvisor review. There's no beach to speak of – just mud. And the whole place stinks! I use the word 'stink' thoughtfully, because 'smell' doesn't do justice to the rank odour of decay that hangs dankly over the entire area. And even though there are a number of pools, you'd want to avoid them, because they're all filled with foul water, an oily sheen on the surface of each.

Perhaps the biggest problem is the constant noise. People enjoy a drink, and so the din of breaking glass is continuous. But despite all of these undeniable challenges, this is a destination that brings great peace to me.

It's our local city rubbish dump. Living in the country, we don't have a refuse collection service – hence the need for my weekly excursion. Anticipation builds as I trundle along, my car loaded. I've carefully sorted the items for recycling, anticipating a new birth for each sheet of cardboard, each bottle and container. But the best thing is this: smelly black refuse sacks, all filled to the brim, jostle in the back of my car, staining the air. I'm looking forward to bidding them farewell.

And then comes the glorious moment. Glass goes into this bin, paper and plastic in that one – but the real elation comes as I finally toss those bursting sacks into the dumpster. They are gone from me forever. I drive home elated, lighter, my rubbish banished, my clutter cleared. I have dumped my trash. But sometimes I don't find some of the other rubbish that I have accumulated quite so straightforward to offload. I insist on carting around sackfuls of shame, gradually collected throughout my personal history. The burden of hauling those emotional bin-bags around can be overwhelming; the stifling smell of regret mingled with remorse and embarrassment fills my nostrils.

The gospel is good news – an invitation to everyone everywhere to offload the heavy weight of their shame onto a heavenly dustman. Jesus took out our trash – to a cross. In a way that I cannot begin to explain, at a flyblown execution site, He took out my sin, and yours.

What a relief it is to offload our greatest regrets, the thoughts and actions that make us blush as we recall them, to dump it all with gratitude upon Him. All are invited, at no cost, to receive forgiveness made possible through that cross.

And this invitation to grace is no luxury, but an absolute necessity. The world has been damaged irreparably by unresolved shame. It nudged Friedrich Nietzsche (famous for his 'God is dead' statement) to declare war on God, because the idea of divinity made him feel like effluent trash: 'He saw with eyes that saw everything… all my concealed disgrace and ugliness… he crawled into my dirtiest nooks. This most curious one had to die.'[1]

But receiving forgiveness is a more subtle art than visiting the city dump. It takes an act of faith to toss my rubbish in Jesus' direction. And there's a ludicrous temptation to refuse mercy, hug my shame close, retrieve those rancid bags, and take them home with me once again, a dark, accusing voice loud in my ears. Perhaps that's one reason for our being given physical tokens – like bread and wine shared – as tangible expressions of grace; receipts of forgiveness.

Today, if your rubbish makes you feel like rubbish, visit the municipal dump. It's located just outside the city wall, on a green hill far away.

[1]Friedrich Nietzsche, 'Thus Spoke Zarathustra', *The Portable Nietzsche* (ed. Walkter Kaufmann) (New York, USA: 1975), p379.

20

Living out loud

The dive master surveyed the nervous gaggle of divers, which included me. He knew we were all scared, and seemed quite delighted about it. We were about to conquer the depths of the Australian Great Barrier Reef. Diving always feels cumbersome until you get into the weightless world of the sea. You clamber around the boat, a heavy oxygen tank on your back, your feet cocooned in ungainly fins (great for swimming, useless for walking). And we had additional encumbrances – we were all trussed up in stinger suits, an underwater body bag that covers virtually all skin, a precaution against box jellyfish.

You don't want to meet a box jellyfish.

A minuscule but pathologically aggressive little critter, this jellyfish, otherwise known as *Chironex fleckeri*, is rather well endowed, with no less than eight gonads and 24 eyes. Their sting produces agonising pain and is reckoned to kill around a hundred people a year. Just recently, two French divers died while exploring the Great Barrier Reef, and the prime suspects are those box jellyfish – both men died from cardiac arrest, a reaction frequently caused by their sting. When the news broke, it emerged that, some years ago, one medical investigator deliberately allowed himself to be stung, in order to understand the power of their venom first-hand. He's a braver man than I, because it appears that they pack a punch a hundred times more powerful than a cobra, and a thousand times greater than a tarantula. Not good.

And this was not the only danger lurking below.

There were sharks.

The dive master, thoroughly enjoying himself now, said that in this stretch of ocean, sharks were *expected*, not just anticipated. Suddenly, the theme music from *Jaws* began playing in my head as I imagined a gang of Great Whites waiting just beneath the surface, all saying grace, giving thanks for the delicious food that was about to be served. Me.

I'd been feeling adventurous. Out hiking the day before, we'd almost stepped on a super-venomous brown snake. We'd parachuted off a cliff, strapped to grinning college students, and landed in a school playground – during the mid-morning break. Apparently, with scant regard for health and safety regulations, the children knew when to get out of the way. Very reassuring.

And then, on safari in the Queensland rainforest, we'd heard about spiders the size of twelve-inch pizzas that drop out of the trees and particularly enjoy attaching themselves to one's face. On top of this, there's the cassowary – an ostrich-like creature with a serious attitude problem –

that has been known to literally disembowel humans they encounter. Call me sentimental, but I like my bowels, and don't want to donate them to a passing bad-tempered bird.

Despite all that I've mentioned, I'm not addicted to danger. But I'd still signed up for the dive, and now, bobbing around on the surface, waiting for the signal to descend, my mind was screaming. I very much wanted to cancel this mad expedition. It didn't matter that I'd paid for it. The thought of staring into the cold, black eyes of a shark or the multitudinous eyes of a toxic jelly fish just didn't appeal. But I didn't signal my change of mind, or climb back into the boat. I dived. There *were* sharks, but, thankfully, they weren't in the mood for a snack. No jellyfish wafted our way.

I learned a stinging truth about myself in that moment, and one that I'm embarrassed to admit. I submerged only because I was anxious what about my fellow divers would think of me, even though I would never see them again once the dive was over. That anxiety outweighed my concern about aquatic predators. Essentially, I went through with it for one reason only: I was driven by the potential opinions of strangers.

I'm not suggesting that we adopt a universal 'not bovvered' approach to life. Only a sociopath doesn't care. But fear of the opinions of others robs us. We decide not to bop around at that wedding reception, worried that our clumsy moves might raise a silent titter with our strictly non-Strictly strutting. In discussions, we back away from saying what we think, worried that we might seem foolish, divisive, opinionated, or all of the above. Leaders obsessed with what others think refuse to make difficult or potentially unpopular decisions, terrified that some will like them less because of their stand.

But neurotic anxiety about the verdicts of others is irrational. Most of the time we won't know what they think, because they won't tell us. So it may surprise us to know that the minds of those around us are elsewhere, and not focused on us at all. As Ethel Barrett said, 'We would worry less about what others think of us if we realised how seldom they do.'

And if they do disapprove, and they're wrong in their judgment, we need to ignore them. Faced with a mounting clamour of criticism from the Pharisees and their pals, Jesus modelled a calm indifference to their snide asides, and quite literally kept calm and carried on.

So when we're tempted to be paralysed with fear about what people think, let's think again, and live out loud anyway.

21

A rite of passage

Clutching my ticket for a brief jaunt on the London Underground, I squeezed myself into an already crammed carriage (the joys of rush hour) and grabbed hold of one of those dangling straps. My journey would be brief – through just five stations – but memorable. I hadn't anticipated that I was about to navigate a rite of passage.

A striking Muslim lady sat nearby. She smiled up at me, and then stood, uttering a sentence that froze my soul: 'Please, sir, do please sit down. Have my seat.'

What? I checked behind me to make sure that she was not being charitable to a slight, bandy-legged 97-year-old who must surely be lurking close by. But she was speaking to *me*. In a millisecond, the horror of the moment broke over me. Apparently I have become that poor old chap who looks like he's going to collapse at any moment; the frail-looking pensioner that younger people might offer a seat to. I stammered my thanks, but added a polite refusal. Not only was I perfectly able to stand, but this was a woman offering her seat to me, a man. I'm not ancient, but I am old enough to remember a time when gentlemen offered their train seats to ladies (although I'm never sure if that's culturally acceptable these days – one may risk being slapped around the head with a copy of a large book by Germaine Greer).

Having muttered my 'thanks but no thanks' reply, I discovered the lady was determined in her politeness: 'No, please – I insist – have my seat.' And with that she moved away, down the carriage. Further refusal would be churlish. I sat down, feeling 20 years older.

Looking across the carriage at my own reflection in the window, I realised that an aging man was staring back at me. I used to have a lot of hair, and had even had it permed in the past, forming a ridiculous canopy that might have gotten me work as a temporary bus shelter. But now the grey has driven the brown away, and what's left of my hair forms a symbolic, stranded peninsula.

It's jet lag, I told myself, *that's why I look older today.* But my last flight had been more than a week prior, so that explanation wouldn't fly (literally).

Desperately, I wondered if her faith had anything to do with her offer. Was there something in the Koran about giving up a seat on a train for strangers?

In the end, I decided to just be glad and grateful. A big city like London can be an emotional wasteland, where thoughtfulness and kindness are as scarce as oxygen on

Mars. This lady's gracious action was lovely – and thought provoking.

As I sat there musing, the train relentlessly carrying me through those tunnels towards my destination, I realised: fighting getting older is useless. It's where all of us are headed, if we're spared to live long enough to see that season. So why not celebrate it, rather than dread it?

As Christians, we hold a Bible that honours the elderly, and never dismisses them. Yet ageism still rears its ugly head in the Church. I know – I've contributed to it in days gone by. My skin crawls as I remember making disparaging remarks about one church during a sermon, insisting that there were only 'three old ladies and a dead cat' in the congregation. Stunningly, it didn't occur to me at the time that lining up elderly females with a deceased feline was hardly respectful, and obviously hurtful.

So I've made a decision (one I'll surely have to reaffirm again and again): getting older is something I'll try to embrace, not fight. I'll neither hanker for the past, nor dread the future, but endeavour to live fully in the now. We who follow Jesus live in the paradox of being a people committed to live one day at a time, yet with an eternity that has no horizon stretching before us. Unwittingly, the polite lady on the Tube had given me more than a seat for five minutes – she had nudged me towards a helpful shift in attitude.

And it was then that I glanced across at my own reflection in the window again. That same aging chap stared back at me still.

But now, he was smiling.

22

What not to say...

It's challenging, and even heartbreaking. A Christian friend confides, sometimes with furtive whispers, that they've been feeling really low; that they're wondering if they're clinically depressed. Would you please pray for them, and do you have any advice? And then comes that awkward silence, where you feel compelled to say something – *anything* – that might be of help. You didn't mean to be clumsy, to palm them off with a cheesy slogan. But before you even had time to say 'cliché', one popped right out of your mouth.

Remember that intentional, focused listening can be more helpful than just saying things with the hope or even expectation that we can 'fix' everything for a depressed person. Your interest, compassion, presence and care matter more than any words that you might say. Remember the advice that comes, not from the book of Proverbs, but from

Ronan Keating. Sometimes, we say it best when we say nothing at all.

But when it comes to what we say, here are five possibilities that will likely make your friend even more depressed than they already are. If you don't want to qualify as a 'friend of Job' (and those guys were seriously unhelpful), avoid these oft-used remarks:

1. 'Get over it'
If they could, they would. That's the point. People don't decide to be depressed, any more than a victim chooses to get attacked. While a depressed person might well need a very gentle nudge to take some action (see a doctor, consider medication, consider diet and exercise, reflect on sleep patterns), what they don't need is an aggressive cheerleader with a megaphone hollering, 'Get a life!' They *want* a life.

2. 'Come out, in Jesus' name!'
Incredibly, some Christians are rather quick on the draw when it comes to linking satanic attack – even demonic possession – with depression and other mental health issues. Who knows what untold damage has been done by people who, armed and dangerous with the latest book on deliverance, 'try out' their theories on people who are not laboratory rats but priceless human beings. We *are* involved in spiritual warfare at times, and we should all remember that. But suggesting that dark forces are always the source of their darkness is unlikely to help. On the contrary.

3. 'Stir your faith'

There are various examples of people who have been rather famous for their faith (take Elijah, for instance) who experienced low periods, figuratively or literally camped in a cave, and perhaps wanted to do nothing but sleep and possibly stop living. Add to the list the apostle Paul, Jeremiah, Jonah, and, yes, Jesus (note His emotional state in Gethsemane) and you'll see that faith doesn't guarantee exemption from emotional turbulence. Elijah had faith to raise the dead, call down fire from heaven, and control the weather, so he had rather spectacular faith – yet still succumbed to a depressive episode that made him want to give up on everything, including life itself.

Be especially hesitant about telling someone who is low to have more faith, especially if you have not called down fire, controlled the weather, or raised the dead this week (waking a teenager in the morning doesn't count).

4. 'I'm going to be there for you'

It's not that you should never say this, but you should only say it when you really mean it, and you know that you can deliver. Depressed people don't need to add 'let down by friends' to their list of things that are getting them down. Offer support by all means, but make sure that (a) you don't create unrealistic expectations and (b) that you deliver what you promise. This includes the pledge that you're going to be praying for them. If you say it, do it.

5. 'Everything will be fine, you'll see'

There's no guarantee that life is going to get sunnier just because we say it will. Life can be hard, and not everything will always turn out how we want it to. Ask the disciples of Jesus – who, for the most part, ended their lives as martyrs. We're not promised that 'everything will be fine', but we are told that, with God, we're never going to be alone again, regardless of what we feel. We do have hope and help to offer, but let's make sure that it's real.

23

The power of prejudice

Sitting three rows back in an unyielding oak pew, I fidgeted restlessly.

I was in unfamiliar territory, parked as I was in this Anglican church with high ceilings and liturgy. I loved the warm glow of the flickering candles, and the unique scent that lingers in buildings that are nearly a thousand years old, but nonetheless, I felt out of place in a church that was, stylistically, a million miles from my own worship expression of choice.

I'm from the charismatic/Pentecostal zone of planet Church, where sung worship is loud, and frequently led by pre-adolescents who have poured themselves into impossibly tight skinny jeans. Despite feeling like Methuselah in some of these high-octane gatherings, it's what I'm at home with. And so when the parish priest began the service with a parsonical drone that reminded me of a famous *Mr Bean* sketch, I bristled.

As the service continued, my mild irritation morphed into indignant anger. I have come to appreciate liturgy. Sometimes life renders us speechless, so to use the well-worn, life-tested words of others can be enormously helpful, and can be a welcome reprieve from the carefully planned spontaneity of some charismatic gatherings. But now the vicar's voice went into full sing-song mode. I seethed. Why couldn't he use his normal voice?

Momentarily feeling guilty for my negative attitude, I quickly justified my inward tut-tutting by telling myself that my anger was righteous; that my frustration came because of my passion for the Church to be relevant.

But I was just being arrogant.

When it was time for the sermon, I braced myself for what would surely be a (hopefully brief) homily of irrelevant twaddle. What happened next was shocking.

The sermon was brilliant. Concise, colourful and relevant, it was a work of verbal art. But even more shocking was my response to this homiletical brilliance.

I hated it. It irked me because my foregone conclusions were so wrong. I so wanted to know that my judgment was right.

Prejudice does that. It looks for confirmation that we are correct, and blinds us to any contradiction that might show our hypothesis about others to be wrong. When someone acts consistently with our blinkered view of them, we gladly nod, happy to be proven right, if only to ourselves. And when they do something that is contrary to what we've decided about them, we tend not to notice it (and if we do, we write it off it as irrelevant; an out of character, one-off aberration).

And then prejudice can cause Christians to be very adept at using labels. Someone steps up with a view (or even a question) that conflicts with our cherished convictions, and before even bothering to dialogue, we write them off by labelling them as being part of *that* group (and they're *so* wrong), which is inferior to *our* group (because we're unfailingly right). Meaningful conversation is silenced, and we hunker down in the trenches of our own opinions.

Jesus was on the receiving end of this blinded thinking. Despite the miracles and wonders that He performed, some of the religious barons of His day didn't seem to notice them, and were only interested in criticising Him because they saw Him as a threat. And even when the miracles were simply undeniable (because chronically ill people were made whole, or dead folks like Lazarus were suddenly alive and hungry for lunch), the only recourse for Jesus' critics was to insist that He was operating with dark powers.

The priest with the parsonical voice proved me wrong. Ashamed, I thought about apologising to him, and then decided that would be unhelpful. I've got a varied collection of bruises from Christians who have 'confessed' to me: they've hated me for years, they say – will I forgive them? Having unburdened themselves, they've walked away relieved, leaving me depressed at knowledge I just didn't need. And so as we filed out of the church, receiving the customary vicarish handshake goodbye, I thanked the priest (perhaps a little too enthusiastically) for his wonderful sermon.

He smiled, and wished me a good day, using his normal voice.

But by then, thankfully, it didn't matter which voice he used.

24

Together

'You're doing *what*?'

My interrogator, his voice shrill and appalled, his nose wrinkled with disdain, stared at me with a mixture of shock and pity.

I repeated my plans for Easter, which involved spending three weeks at an annual Christian event where the Harvest is brought in during Spring. He shook his head in disbelief, as if I'd just revealed plans to kill my own grandmother. 'What a total waste of time,' he muttered. 'Those big events are just mindless jamborees for Christians. Come the revolution, I'd cancel 'em all.'

But he couldn't have been more wrong. I've spent a lot of time – years, cumulatively, over the last four decades – attending, contributing and helping organise camps, retreats and conferences. As it happens, I'm writing this while en route to yet another one. And my experiences have led me to this conclusion: God is an event planner.

Feasts and festivals have long been on His calendar, not only *inviting* His people to gather for lengthy bashes, like the Feasts of Pentecost, Passover, and Weeks, but actually *commanding* them to show up.

Those non-optional parties were disruptive and cost a lot of time and money (especially in a culture where first class travel was an athletic donkey). National celebrations were colourful and creative. During the Feast of Tabernacles, the people of Israel didn't just rehearse the story of the Exodus with words spoken, but actually relived the experience, camping out in temporary shelters for a week. And the feasts were far from solemn gatherings of the frozen chosen. God made fun compulsory, hence this rather surprising command about an offering in Deuteronomy:

'Use the silver to buy whatever you like: cattle, sheep, wine or other fermented drink, or anything you wish. Then you and your household shall eat there in the presence of the LORD your God and rejoice' (Deut. 14:26).

In my early years as a Christian, youth camps galvanised my fledgling faith. Admittedly, I was a bit overenthusiastic, and went forward in response at the end of every sermon, occasionally repenting of things that weren't even sin. My calling in life was confirmed during another youth weekend. And during 30 years of involvement with the afore-hinted Spring Harvest, I learned some vital truths:

- There really were Christians in other denominational tribes apart from my own.
- My way of doing faith wasn't the only way, or even the best way – which came as quite a surprise.

- Strength can come from worshipping in a large gathering of believers.
- It's possible to disagree agreeably, and have intelligent conversations about issues that are usually contentious.

But most of all, these events have helped me to remember: to recall who God is, and remember who I am, too. I've never lost my faith, but I do occasionally mislay it.

One of the most oft-repeated complaints from God about His people, particularly in the Old Testament, is simply this: *they forgot*.

And so the festivals nudged everyone to remember, and sat alongside other strategies for identity recall (such as circumcision for the chaps – rather alarming, given the lack of anaesthetic at the time). These strategies worked, and they still do.

When we get together, sing our songs, pray our prayers, and open the Book, we remember just exactly why we have a pulse, and Who gave it to us. In the blur of information overload (where we post far too many unnecessary photos on social media and know a great deal too much about the mundane details of each other's lives) these events enable us to bring to mind what really does matter. We recall our covenant with God again, and consider how we're doing with our end of the bargain.

And these days, there are plenty of options to choose from. I won't list them, but if you can, go ahead: head for a tent, a chalet, a retreat centre, or a conference. If you do, I pray your faith will be rebooted, your mind stretched, and your heart opened to new friendships. Perhaps it might even be the tiniest taste of what forever will look like, because, come the ultimate kingdom revolution, when Christ comes and every knee bows, it's where we'll all be.

Together.

25

Here is the news

It was an unexpected invitation.

Staying at a hotel in Jerusalem, we were a group of 120 wide-eyed pilgrims, keen to not only see the biblical sites but also to wrestle with the complex issues that make the Holy Land a cauldron of turmoil. I'm not terribly impacted by revered locations (it matters not to me that this was the mountain where Moses supposedly paused for elevenses) but I enjoy the rustic beauty of Galilee, as well as standing on the worn steps of the Temple, near where Jesus turned the tables. The ancient ruins of Capernaum are a personal favourite, even if a rather monstrous building has been built over the remains of what is thought to be Peter's house, which seems rather rude. Some of our group had been baptised in the Jordan, despite the brown, muddy water and passing catfish that were keen for a nibble of human snacks that came wrapped in white gowns.

We'd heard impassioned presentations from Jewish tour guides, insisting that in a post-holocaust world, the land was surely theirs. We visited Bethlehem, now encircled by a wall twice the size of the one that once spliced Berlin, and heard from Palestinian Christians who felt bullied and forgotten by the wider world, especially the Church world.

And then came an unexpected invitation to Gary, one of our group. A security specialist from Northern Ireland, he is more aware than most of the dangers of unfamiliar territory. But he and a Palestinian member of the hotel staff had struck up a conversation about football. The waiter proffered an offer: would Gary and a couple of friends like to go to his home to watch the game that was airing that evening?

Responding was not without risk, for both parties. Gary and his mates could have been walking into a trap, for all they knew. And the Palestinian ran the risk of being seen fraternising with those outside of their community, potentially arousing suspicion. But the evening turned out beautifully. Gary and his friends were treated as guests of honour – a cake had been baked, and trust was celebrated as people forgot nationality and ethnicity, and settled down to just be members of the human family together.

In sharing this story, my intention is not to comment on the political situation in the Holy Land. But it is just heartwarming to hear of people taking risks to connect across perceived divides. Stereotypes are shattered, prejudice is eroded, and hope is birthed.

Just this week I heard about another wondrous invitation. Hugh was raised in a loving but staunch unionist family in Ulster. Enmity can blossom early; he recalls dodging stones hurled by Catholic kids as he walked to school in the mornings. His response was to make regular hit and run skirmishes up Seaforde Street, a republican stronghold and flashpoint marooned in the middle of Protestant East Belfast, smashing the windows of those he viewed as enemies. On that street was a chapel where IRA snipers had crouched.

But then, years later, as an adult and pastor, Hugh had been invited to participate in a funeral in that very same chapel. Wondering if anyone might recognise him from his window-smashing days, he attended, and was then asked to be a pallbearer to carry the coffin of someone's Catholic son. So he obliged, lending his shoulder in the solemn cortège that edged down Seaforde Street. And as he walked, ever so slowly in contrast to his vandal-esque sprinting from years gone by, he realised how much his own heart had changed over the decades.

The point of these two stories? There is none, except that I offer them as a tiny trickle against the flood of bad news that so often dominates our headlines. As we have rightly wept over atrocities in Iraq, Somalia, Syria and elsewhere, as we have been horrified by the callous slaughter of a priest at his own altar, our response might not just be one of compassion, solidarity and prayer, but of fear and even despair.

But in the midst of the darkness, there is light, and around the world today, not only will kingdom people be quietly making a difference, but human beings of all faiths and none will be kind, respectful, generous; taking faltering, risky steps of love.

And that is surely enough to make these stories worth telling.

26

Waiting

It's one of my least favourite things to do. I go to the supermarket, head for the cheese counter, and take one of those numbers helpfully dispensed to prevent irate shoppers from punching each other if someone jumps the queue. My number is 451. The digital readout indicates that they are serving customer number 47. I hope that cheese sandwich is worth the waiting.

I call my mobile phone company, and am greeted by a robotic voice inviting me to press 1 for this, 2 for that. Rapidly I move through layers of numeric choices, but then, I wait. I listen to music apparently composed by a deranged person. Sometimes I am informed of my whereabouts in the queue and how long I can expect to be on hold (a strategy to keep me hopeful, perhaps). Then, at last, I am greeted by an actual human and we play a little quiz together, otherwise known as *Answering the Security Questions*. What's my mother's maiden name, and my pet's favourite colour?

And then, the ultimate test – the one that sends fear trembling through my very being – what is my password?

Technology has eased much of our waiting. Older readers will recall the demonic invention known as dial-up networking – a torturous method of accessing the internet. The computer made endless electronic spluttering noises and after an eternity (well, 20 seconds at least) the modem would eventually connect. For most, those days have gone. We're increasingly used to everything being fast; instant; high speed. Waiting isn't our natural posture.

And then we come to God, who is the Blesser, but is not a fibre-optic deity. God is in no hurry. Dashing is not His style, as Jesus demonstrated continually.

Methodically, He walked His disciples slowly through scenarios of learning, and then spent six whole weeks with them *after* the resurrection, painstakingly reiterating kingdom truths, shaping them to be world-changers.

And then He gave one final command before the Ascension:

Wait.

Don't head for home, back to the anonymity, the relative safety of Galilee.

No – stay put in Jerusalem, the big, dangerous city where, just a few weeks earlier, He, their leader, had been tortured and executed. It was perilous territory still, and a ten-day waiting period to come. Perhaps the waiting was deliberately designed to fuel dependency; to know how desperately they needed the Holy Spirit to help them. And surely there was some calendar choreography here – the Day of Pentecost was a celebration of fulfilment. Not only was the harvest safely gathered in, but the nation remembered the giving of the Law to Moses. It was surely an appropriate day for the giving of the Spirit.

Whatever the reason, for the disciples, waiting was a prelude to power. It often is. But that doesn't make waiting any more palatable.

Prayer usually nudges me into a waiting room. As I bow my head and mutter heavenward, I ask God a question, and most of the time I am greeted by silence (by 'most', I mean 99.99999% of the time).

Suffering calls for waiting. Today I sat with two epically brave souls who are waiting patiently in line. Les and Marsha are wonderful Christians, and they're in the thick of a horrendous battle with cancer. A shadow of the man he was, Les is wheelchair-bound and hooked up to oxygen. The tumours in his neck are outraged at the fight he's putting up. Sometimes Les wakes up screaming in unbearable pain, and the morphine ('enough to drop a horse,' says Marsha) isn't winning. Les isn't afraid of dying – that's the least of his problems. 'It's the thought of this pain getting even worse that scares the hell out of me,' he confesses. Sitting with them in the oncology department of the local hospital, I bow my head in their presence, partly to hide my tears, but also as a gesture of humility before their honest, gutsy trust. And I am just a little bit angry – frustrated at those who insist that healing is always on tap immediately for those who can summon up enough faith.

So today, let's remember all who wait – for that elusive

healing to come, for prodigals to head homeward, for answers to questions that gnaw at their days and fill their sleepless nights. And if you are among that brave throng, may you be strengthened in your waiting, and while the flame of hope surely flickers at times, may it never be snuffed out.

27

The meeting

I spend a good chunk of my life attending Christian services and meetings.

In my home church, we have multiple services every weekend. When I'm preaching, I get to share the same sermon *four* times – the same outline, points, the same 'spontaneous' humour, repeatedly. I get the joy of listening, and often remark to my wife, Kay, that I get sick of the sound of my own voice.

Smiling, she replies, 'I completely understand how you feel.'

I've been in so many 'times of worship' in the last 50 years that, based on my calculations, I reckon I have sung one rather overused song for the equivalent of no less than three months, and have spent nearly a year of my life with my hands raised. (OK, I made those stats up.)

Itinerant ministry has granted me the privilege of seeing the church in a myriad of tribal variations. I've coughed reverently in the presence of incense-swinging Anglo-Catholics, attempted to dance along with some breathlessly high-spirited charismatics (I was just breathless), and enjoyed a week with some Irish Methodists, who didn't drink alcohol, being Methodists, but if eating puddings was an Olympic event, they'd have the Gold in the bag. I've enjoyed the oom-pah-pah of brass bands with Australian Salvationists, and joined the collective chorus of vibrant gospel churches in London.

But out of all of these thousands of services, there is just one that stands out as the most remarkable. It happened nearly thirty years ago, but was so memorable that, decades later, I still meet people who whimsically say, 'I was there that night.'

I was the speaker, although I didn't get to say much.

It all began when, while walking to the tent where something like a thousand young people were gathered, I heard God whisper to me, 'Tonight, I'm going to teach you a lesson that you'll never, ever forget.'

This piqued my interest. God doesn't speak to me a lot – at least, not in my assessment. I was due to preach on the power of the Holy Spirit, and had planned to begin my talk with a simple illustration of fatherhood. It's the loving Father who gives us the gifts of the Holy Spirit, and when we feel safe with Him, we're more likely to be open to His power. My then two-year-old son Richard would toddle out onto the platform, and I would hold him in my arms for a minute or two, while talking about how secure he was with me as his dad. That was it.

The worship band played quietly. Then Richard suddenly threw his arms back, and for a moment, it looked like he was going to punch me (which would have been awkward – the sight of me with a bloodied nose would have somewhat spoiled the illustration of warm father–son affection). But instead, he wrapped his arms tightly around me, and buried his head in my neck.

It was then that it happened.

People suddenly fell to the ground, instantly succumbing to the wave of the Holy Spirit that filled the tent. Others cried out, a response to the sense of unfathomable awe that pervaded. And within minutes, as Richard and I just stood there, a queue of people formed – folks who had all been instantly healed in that moment. No one asked them to come forward, they just came.

I tried to preach, without success. I'm not into the 'God moved so powerfully, the sermon was cancelled' notion. Biblical teaching matters. But that night, it was placed on hold.

And the lesson I learned? It is, as Jim Packer once said, that the alphabet of Christianity begins with 'F' for 'Father'.

How should we pray? Start with, 'Our Father'.

How should we die? Use the Jewish night prayer, 'Into your hands I commend my Spirit,' but do what Jesus did while on the cross, in an action that was revolutionary. Preface the prayer with 'Father'.

And for those who tragically have had a negative, even abusive experience of fatherhood, may you find comfort in the truth that Jesus never said that God is like your dad.

Rather, He taught that God is like no other father that we've ever known. Resting in His Fatherhood doesn't just come naturally to any of us. According to the Book, the Holy Spirit wants to work in our hearts, enabling us to cry 'Abba', and rest in the Father's love.

It was a life-altering lesson, yet one that will take eternity to fully learn.

He's a good, good Father.

28

A little means a lot

When Ken showed up at church, he caused quite a stir. Some of our congregation, concerned about their safety, called upon the Lord with a whispered prayer for protection. Others, preferring more temporal security, considered calling the police.

We don't normally treat visitors with such suspicion, but Ken was the ultimate portrait of menace. Dressed totally in black, with his arms and face covered in some pretty interesting tattoos, his studded trench coat made him look like a vampire – and some of our congregation weren't keen on giving blood. His rage was further confirmed by his tattooed knuckles. On one hand, a four-letter word that began with 'F' was scrawled. And on the other, to complete the abusive greeting, was the word 'you!'

That had been Ken's lifelong message.

An angry drug abuser who had spent more than half of his life in jail, he was notorious in the community, his face permanently twisted into a snarl. He only came to the service because someone dared him to attend. 'You're so horrible, you should try church,' they had said. Hardly a warm evangelistic strategy, but it had apparently worked.

Ken sat at the back, absolutely determined to be unmoved, and later confessed that in his living memory, he had never, ever cried. Who knows what horrible childhood traumas had smitten his tear ducts with a lifelong drought?

Then little Marge Sample showed up. Silver-haired, elderly, and with a smile that could light up a room, diminutive Marge was on duty as a member of the welcome team that morning. She boldly strolled over to where Ken was sitting, his arms folded defiantly.

'Hello!' she chirped. 'I'm Marge. I don't believe we've met?' She rested her hand lightly on his studded shoulder.

Marge was somewhat taken aback by Ken's immediate, violent response. Burying his face in his hands, he suddenly exploded into loud wailing. This was no penitent whimper: he howled. Heads turned nervously.

Ken sobbed his way into the kingdom that day. The emotional dam-burst was triggered, quite simply, because for the first time in a very long time, someone had been pleased to see him. A simple gesture of welcoming kindness unlocked a man who had been imprisoned by hate for decades.

Ken started to attend church, and his enthusiasm in worship initially caused a few raised eyebrows. When he raised his hands in praise, people three rows back got a rather unexpected message from those lifted knuckles! So eventually, Ken decided to have that lettering removed by laser surgery. A doctor in the church volunteered his time, and we took an offering to cover other hospitalisation costs. Standing in the baptismal tank with his hands still encased in post-operation plastic bags, he thanked the congregation. His face beaming, he held up those hands.

'Now the outside matches the inside,' he said, 'I'm clean.'

Ken's life was totally transformed, and his conversion stuck.

Sometimes it doesn't take a lot to change everything.

Marge passed away just last night, her sparkling eyes now just a memory, at least for the time being. But she's living proof that small acts of kindness can trigger revolution. And who knows? Perhaps, last night, when she found herself in the presence of a heavenly welcoming committee, another Someone with hands wounded – not by hate, but by love – stepped forward with a smile.

More stories and wisdom from Jeff Lucas

The Cactus Stabbers

Jeff tells the intriguing stories of characters he has met while travelling around the world. He makes you think as he looks at life through his realistic, yet invariably optimistic, lenses.
ISBN: 978-1-78259-327-0

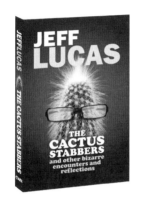

I Was Just Wandering...

Jeff describes embarrassing mishaps, struggles and laugh-out-loud episodes from his own life as he offers relief by reminding us that we're not alone.
ISBN: 978-1-85345-850-7

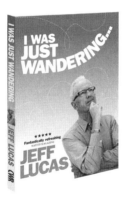

As well as these, there is a whole range of books and DVDs by Jeff Lucas for you to explore.

For current prices or to order, visit **www.cwr.org.uk/store**
Available online or from Christian bookshops.

Be inspired by God.
Every day.

One-year subscriptions available for all titles

Life Every Day

Jeff Lucas will help you gain insight, understanding and practical application from God's Word every day with these bimonthly Bible reading notes.

Every Day with Jesus

Popular daily Bible reading notes by Selwyn Hughes.

Inspiring Women Every Day

Daily insight and encouragement written by women for women.

Cover to Cover Every Day

In-depth study of the Bible, book by book. Part of a five-year series.

To order or subscribe, visit **www.cwr.org.uk/store** or call **01252 784700**.
Also available in Christian bookshops.

 Print subscription available

 **Large Print subscription** available

 Email subscription available

Courses and seminars

Waverley Abbey College

Publishing and media

Conference facilities

Transforming lives

CWR's vision is to enable people to experience personal transformation through applying God's Word to their lives and relationships.

Our Bible-based training and resources help people around the world to:
• Grow in their walk with God
• Understand and apply Scripture to their lives
• Resource themselves and their church
• Develop pastoral care and counselling skills
• Train for leadership
• Strengthen relationships, marriage and family life and much more.

Our insightful writers provide daily Bible reading notes and other resources for all ages, and our experienced course designers and presenters have gained an international reputation for excellence and effectiveness.

CWR's Training and Conference Centres in Surrey and East Sussex, England, provide excellent facilities in idyllic settings – ideal for both learning and spiritual refreshment.

CWR Applying God's Word
to everyday life and relationships

CWR, Waverley Abbey House,
Waverley Lane, Farnham,
Surrey GU9 8EP, UK

Telephone: **+44 (0)1252 784700**
Email: **info@cwr.org.uk**
Website: **www.cwr.org.uk**

Registered Charity No. 294387
Company Registration No. 1990308